I0435750

From Liberty to Caesar

How Our Loss of Personal Choice Will Result in Forced Conformity

By Logan Henry

Copyright 2016 by Logan Henry
All rights reserved. This book or any portions thereof may not be
reproduced or used in any manner whatsoever without
the written permission of Logan Henry, except for
the use of brief quotations in a book review.

ISBN 1530826020

CreateSpace, Charleston SC
Available from Amazon.com and other book stores

One

For the first and only time in history a nation state was created and formed to protect individual liberty. The revolution of the American Colonies of England was generated by ideas that had been circulating for more than 200 years. They were ideas about how best to form a government and upon what grounds to formulate government. None but a few conceived of men living without government, which was considered, and still is considered, among thoughtful people, essential for human welfare.

Some proposed that government was founded upon the will of God, thus they found God as the basis for kings and emperors. Many, however, rejected the idea that God ordained kings. Gradually thoughtful men concluded that the power incipient in the people who support government was the only real basis for a government. As the ideas concerning the basis for government advanced, many also championed the radical idea that the people governed should be left with the greatest liberty of personal choice possible consistent with maintaining order and sovereignty. It was a very radical idea at the time.

It was into this cauldron seething with aspirations for individual liberty and acquisition of personal wealth that Great Britain imposed its power upon a people who had been living at liberty for 125 years. They rebelled. They won their liberty. They first formed a coalition of the Colonies which they called States, but, the coalition government was too weak to survive. Britain, France and Spain waited to conquer the States individually and impose themselves upon the people who had won their independence in bloody battle. Those people came together to create a government dedicated to the preservation of individual liberty. There were still Tories among them. There were also those infected with the ideas that later spawned the French Revolution. Despite views to the contrary they adopted the Constitution of the United States of America in which they attempted to guarantee the blessings of liberty to themselves and to those who came after them.

Some who followed soon began a collectivist assault upon individual liberty and today it has been buried in the rhetoric of collectivism. Equally important, it has been buried in the rhetoric of received opinion. The very idea has vanished. There remain some voices championing religious liberty, freedom of speech, freedom of the press, but none champion individual liberty itself.

Today the media and the press routinely report of the activities of those they call liberals or progressives, and, slightly, libertarians, and those called conservatives. The progressives are in favor of more federal intervention in the market place, greater government expenditures on behalf of the unsuccessful, massive spending on infrastructure, reduced spending on the military, relatively little restrictions on immigration and an easing of incarceration for many crimes. The conservatives are in favor of spending more on the military, restricting abortions, refusing to acknowledge homosexual marriage, repeal of the Affordable Care Act, aggressive foreign policy and reducing federal spending. There are those who seek to provide a way for people who entered the USA illegally to become citizens and those who want them deported. Some debate exists over how best to create jobs and how to deal with terrorists. There is unanimity over the suppression of discrimination and the pursuit of diversity. There are none who raise a voice to notice the erosion of individual liberty in the United States of America. There has been a continuing erosion of individual liberty, presently advancing more rapidly, in the country created to protect individual liberty.

Although the erosion of individual liberty in the United States of America has been a steady stream since the turn of the 20th century, it presents itself as more menacing than ever at present. The voices that are ever before us tell us that inequality of income and wealth must be dealt with or the consequences portend dreadful results. There seems, also, that there is no argument to the contrary. Now, it seems from recent studies, that there is a gap between the life expectancy of those with wealth and those without wealth. Both parties echo the same refrain, that the differences are deplorable. There is a unanimous voice renouncing individual discrimination. The voice is spontaneous and without dissent. Discrimination will not be permitted and something must be done to equalize the distribution of income and wealth. All the while, lawlessness is increasing. Society requires that its citizens be peaceful and law abiding; society will ultimately do what is necessary to suppress lawlessness because it renders living insupportable. At present some of the lawlessness is tolerated as expressions of outrage with inequality. The government will, however, in the long term, suppress everything in order to suppress lawlessness. Meanwhile, lawlessness increases apace. Riots, attacks on peace officers, demands for police restraint in law enforcement, public chants for death to police all have become almost daily events. Lawlessness presents itself in the form of student rebellion against the authorities at universities. Such lawlessness has preceded most tyrannies. Such unanimous received opinion and objection to the distribution of wealth and income has generally preceded the acclamation of a Caesar.

Normally the comments upon inequality of income and wealth condemn the fact. Normally the comments do not tell just how inequality of income comes about. Often the comments point out that many have inadequate educations to perform in today's economy and contend for more expenditure on education. Normally such comments predict that devastating consequences will result from continued inequality. Normally such comments imply, or expressly state, that the means to equalize is by taxation and redistribution. Normally the comments do not mention that forced equalization of income and wealth through taxation necessarily includes a corresponding loss of individual liberty. Normally such comments are silent on the history of the United States that created the only government ever to exist dedicated to individual liberty. Normally such observations are silent regarding the power over the people necessary to equalize them. Normally such comments assume, without argument, that the government has the power to equalize and that equalization would be good, nay, necessary. Lost in the arguments is the precept that power in the government is inimical to individual liberty, an idea commonly accepted at the creation of the United States and carried into the Constitution. There is almost a unanimous agreement condemning the inequality and an outrage at the fact that only a small portion of the population owns an immense portion of the wealth.

The comment about the failure of middle incomes to increase, and the inequality between the middle class and the upper 5 percent includes demands that the government do something to narrow the gap. There is no dissent within the comments about the need, only dissent about the means. People generally believe that the United States government can and should cause incomes to increase. Some programs suggested would also increase the immense debt with which the USA has saddled itself. Many are unconcerned with massive government debt. There will, therefore, be an increase in demand for redistribution. Redistribution is the increasing cry of the "progressives". Redistribution through higher taxes on the successful is now resisted through suggestions that pro business policies will improve the incomes of the middle class. Perhaps pro-business policies will be made law in the near future, but, if they do not close the gap, redistribution will become irresistible. Another step in the loss of individual liberty will have become without a dissenting voice.

Much of the agenda of the "progressives" is salutary when considered alone. Who could not be in favor of help for the poor, the elderly? Who could not be for the elimination of irrational discrimination? Who could not be in favor of quality medical care for all? Problems, however, arise in the inevitable despotism necessary to achieve more equal distribution of income and wealth through government power. The problem also arises in the inevitable inability of the government (the people) to be able to pay for the programs. And, most important of all, the problem presents itself to an informed person, that the power withheld by the Constitution and now relinquished by the people to the Government, will ultimately devolve upon a tyrant, just as it has time and again in the past.

The power withheld by the Constitution and relinquished to the government when used by Congress often results in despotic acts. It has become an ordinary expectation that, regardless of the despotic nature of the actions of the government, that government do something to improve the hopes and aspirations of the people. There exists, and always has existed, an element of people who care but little for other than what government can do for them. That element of society cares but little for liberty, and care dearly for their own needs. That element of society cares but little for individual liberty and often refuse to conform their own conduct and do as they please without concern for the legal restraints which seek to provide a peaceful life within which to work and earn a living. Time and again in history that element of a society has gladly bestowed unlimited power upon one man. That element of society has been joined by those who care more for equalizing society than for individual liberty. That combination of society has delivered the power of government to one man time and again throughout history. When Caesar arrives he always imposes the power of the government upon all and suppresses the free expression of opinion, political activity, all forms of lawlessness and demonstrations. Caesar always promises to care for those who support him.

Caesar always imposes the power of the government upon all in the name of care for the needy.

Because increasing income is the result of the ability to perform in the existing economic circumstances, and because there are many who are unable to perform in today's conditions, the clear danger of the rise of a "strong man" promising to make conditions better is upon us. Quoting from a prominent columnist for The New York Times, "mass democracy seems to demand a single iconic figure into whom desires and aspirations can be poured." Now it is clearly before us that a President can be willing to become a Caesar. Head strong uses of a power to bring about his purposes without regard for the Constitutional separation of power have become daily actions, law by fiat. As pointed out by LeCompte Dunoy, a people who find it necessary to place term limits upon a chief subconsciously concede the willingness to acclaim a Caesar. Another prominent columnist for The New York Times has noted the obvious removal of the vast majority of Americans from the ideas of the classical liberal movement that created the United States of America. Such retreat from the ideas of individual liberty also portends the retreat into increasing government power over the lives of individuals within the jurisdiction of the government.

A clear precursor to a Caesar.

Two

The Constitution as originally written, and for many years, prohibited the imposition of a direct tax upon the citizenry. The framers had seen the power over the people which lay in the government's power to tax. As one Supreme Court justice wrote, "the power to tax is the power to destroy." For many years prior to 1916 the element of society who called themselves "progressives" had campaigned for a direct tax upon incomes. They had taken the idea from a burgeoning population of "Marxists". After several years of clamoring, in 1916, the progressives succeeded and the Constitution was amended to provide for a direct tax upon incomes. In one fell swoop every American became the slave of the government. The government could, by fiat, take all or any part of what any and every American earned. The government was not reticent in using that power and at times since 1916 it has taken, by the power to tax, as much as 90 percent of parts of some incomes. The government now stands at the threshold of confiscation and redistribution of an immense portion of the production of the people of America. It will do so initially in the name of equalization, but, when Caesar arrives it will do so to perpetuate the power of Caesar.

A direct tax upon the estates of the deceased is the cry of those who despise the accumulation of wealth and seek to confiscate wealth in the name of equalization. Such a tax was a touchstone of Marxists among us in the early 20th century. The grasping cry of the "progressives" of today call for the confiscation of estates although they have been frustrated until now. Such confiscation has always been the practice of a Caesar. Such clamoring by the "progressives" cry out that they are more than ready to welcome a Caesar.

The Civil Rights Act of 1964 was intended to eliminate the practice of discrimination. It applied to governmental entities and to corporations and individuals engaged in interstate commerce. At the time there were a few dissenters, but, almost all favored elimination of discrimination. The practice was considered to be detestable and elimination necessary. Many felt that individuals had no right to the detestable practice. The argument that to be discriminating had always been considered virtuous was cast aside with scant notice. The law prohibited Lester Maddox from continuing to operate his cafeteria by serving only those he chose to serve. Prior to the law he was at liberty to operate his business as he chose and refuse service to those he chose. After the law his liberty to so choose was denied. Lester Maddox and all others were denied that liberty. He closed the cafeteria and ran for and was elected Governor of Georgia.

Regardless of the hatefulness of his discrimination toward black people, he was deprived of his individual choice and thus, his individual liberty, and the individual liberty of all was to that extent usurped by government. A right to practice a business and earn a living as one chose so long as he did not harm others was deleted from the law in the United States and the right to demand service from those who practiced a business was substituted. The liberty to discriminate had no place in America.

Today virtually none see the elimination of Lester Maddox's private discrimination as a deprivation of individual liberty. Rather, they see the practice of individual discrimination as too detestable to permit, regardless of its obvious limitation upon individual choice, individual liberty.

Some states and many municipalities have enacted statutes and ordinances which plainly, simply and without apology make it unlawful to discriminate. Thus, obviously, restricting the exercise of individual liberty in the name of elimination of discrimination. The imposition of popular, received, opinion upon individuals has always been a precursor to the elevation of a Caesar.

The US Congress passed a law which prohibits discrimination in hiring. All persons engaged in business lost the individual choice, individual liberty, which they had previously enjoyed by reason of the Constitution of the United States. It is unlikely that any noticeable portion of the people object to the restriction of individual choice embodied in the law.

In the recent past there have been some who refused to be involved in a marriage between two people of the same sex. Some are seeking that the courts impose damages upon the artisans and officials who refused to participate in the homosexual marriage. Recently reported is the ruling of a court that a baker must pay damages because he refused to decorate a cake for a customer involved in a same sex marriage. The court's opinion was that the public's refusal to permit discrimination took precedence over a person's religious beliefs.

Recently Indiana enacted a law which provided protection to individuals and businesses who refused service on the grounds of heartfelt religious beliefs. An immense negative reaction to the law arose. The Governor and Legislature capitulated to the criticism. The complaint against the law was that it might lead to discrimination against homosexuals. The unanimous reaction regardless of a position on the law has been to condemn discrimination. Though no harm has been demonstrated to those the object of discrimination, other than hurt feelings, it has apparently become received opinion that discrimination must be punished, nay, eliminated. The baker, along with many others, has been deprived of his liberty. Some object to his punishment on the grounds of an infringement of religious liberty. No voice has been raised in defense of individual liberty.

It has now become likely that mere hurt feelings might be considered sufficient damage to support the suppression of discrimination and the award of money damages for those hurt feelings arising from discrimination. The New York Times reports that many people equate discrimination with harm.

When public opinion has become so coalesced against individual actions that do no harm, other than hurt feelings, and when hurt feelings can become considered to be damage just as physical harm, there is no limit to the restrictions that may be imposed upon individuals. Received opinions are inimical to individual liberty. Those who declaim and shout may find themselves punished, indeed, should they call for the individual liberty to discriminate, while doing no harm, they will suffer. Anti discrimination laws are but a harbinger of greater inroads into individual liberty and a forthcoming welcome to Caesar. Few realize that when Caesar presented himself to Rome as an unlimited tyrant, though he covered it with humility, he was welcomed. When a later Caesar attempted to return power to the Senate they refused to accept.

The Affordable Health Care Act provides that those who might choose to not buy health insurance must buy health insurance or face a fine. Should such a person choose to not buy insurance and then not pay the financial penalty, he or she would, inescapably, ultimately, be imprisoned for not paying the fine.

Buy insurance or go to jail.

Such people are deprived of their individual liberty in order that some others, theretofore uninsurable, become insured. It has been found to be constitutional, but, it is none the less despotic when considered from the standpoint of the individual. Many felt that liberty to, and responsibility for, care only for oneself had no place in America.

When public opinion has so coalesced as to prohibit individuals from caring for themselves alone, only collectives will be accorded rights. Individual rights are in clear jeopardy.

There are other aspects of The Affordable Care Act that are despotic, when viewed from the standpoint of individuals. Until its passage those who led healthy lives were offered policies by insurance companies that refused to insure those who led unhealthy lives thus having insurance at lower costs for those who lead healthy lives. There were policies available that did not include obstetric care. Many have no need for obstetric care. Such policies were less costly for those who had no need for obstetric care. Those policies are prohibited by the affordable care act. Those who live healthy lives and those who have no need for obstetric care are forced to pay for policies that provide coverage for those who do not lead healthy lives and for those who want obstetric care.

Many felt that liberty to provide for oneself alone had no place in America, therefore those who lead healthy lives are forced to pay for care for those who abuse their bodies. Those who do not smoke are forced to pay for care for those who smoke. Those who keep their weight under control are forced to pay for care for those who are obese. Those who do not use dangerous drugs are forced to pay for care for those who do use such drugs. Those who use alcoholic beverages in moderation, or not at all, are forced to pay for care for those who abuse alcohol. The cost of health insurance has consequently become greater, and increases apace. Even with increases in premiums it is reported that some of the insurance companies are losing money at such a rate that they are refusing to provide coverage.

Mr. Filburn sought to grow wheat for his own consumption but he was prohibited by an act of Congress intended to stabilize the price of wheat.

Perhaps it is better for society to force conformation to higher purposes, as seen by some, than personal choice. Is society better off when individual choice is subverted to popular demand, to the needs of others? That question has always been answered in the affirmative by those who seek a society which conforms to their view of what is right, what is good, what is best for many, to those who refuse to tolerate deviation from their view of what is best. That is a view which has always been rejected by those who seek a society which permits an individual to choose his own course so long as he does not harm others. Under a government powerful enough to force individual choice, none are removed from its tentacles, no forced action is prohibited. The United States of America was conceived in the protection of individual liberty and, thus, limited the power of the government. That limited government has been superseded by a government unlimited in its power over the people. Such a society will find it easy and natural to accept, gladly welcome, a Caesar.

Three

We have historical examples of both views. The United States of America from its inception until the turn of the 20th Century, and to an extent, for a while thereafter, chose individual liberty. Russia from its inception to the present has permitted individual choice only so long as it comports with government mandates. Russia, from Czars to Politburo to President and Parliament has, without restraint, imposed its view upon individuals. Russia has been a very bad place for most of its citizens. The United States has always been a good place for its citizens, but, it is slipping into despotism. The United States is in the process of abandoning any retention of individual liberty as we collectively impose upon the people the choice of government over the choice of individuals, the choice of activist groups over the choice of individuals. The origins of the USA were quite different. The Constitutional Convention of 1787 attempted to create a government with limited power in order to protect individual liberty.

Webster's Collegiate Dictionary 1961 defines slave as:
*One whose person and services are under the
control of another as owner or master.*

The essence of slavery is that the fruits and benefits of one's labor and thought are enjoyed by another. There would have never been a slave but for that very essence.

People work to have food, shelter, clothes, entertainment, education, and a certain amount of leisure. The fruits and benefits of that work amount to they themselves, just in a different form.

To repeat for emphasis: The fruits and benefits of a person's work are that person. An exchange took place. An equation occurred, part of that person for those fruits and benefits. Those fruits and benefits become that person.

When a portion of those fruits and benefits are voluntarily relinquished an act of sovereign individuality occurs. When a portion of those fruits and benefits are forcibly taken those people are become as slaves.

A Roman slave routinely labored to produce farm crops, cooked food, clean clothes, clean premises, transportation, and, in certain families, personal protection and instruction. They were housed, fed, clothed and permitted some leisure time. In many households they occupied privileged status, though remaining a slave. The government of the United States of America forcibly takes a portion of the fruits and benefits of the labor of its people and permits them to retain a portion for housing, food, clothing and a bit of leisure. Until now the Congress has imposed a limit upon itself because it has feared the electorate. For a time some incomes were functionally expropriated but that became unpopular. It may no longer be unpopular.

Taxes, when directed toward essential governmental actions amount to fruits and benefits voluntarily relinquished. When directed to governmental actions that do not protect and defend those who pay the taxes, to that extent those who are so taxed are become as slaves. It is not hard for those with much less to care but little for the expropriation of money from those who profit immensely. So long as the exercise of the power is thus restricted it will be popular. It has never been permanently so restricted, and now we can see the creep of despotic power. That power, when it has reached the limits of the coffers of the 1 percent, will, as it always has, take in 5 percent, 10 percent, 20 percent until it has become, as the Soviet Union, all people except the rulers themselves. The Affordable Care Act is obvious, but many others exist. The press reports that the welfare state is popular. No such reports are seen regarding the protection of individual liberty.

Four

Trade to gain the necessary items of life is conducted in a medium called money. Until recently money existed as a commodity such as gold, silver, copper, sea shells etc. Often a king took, cut off, a portion of a coin which then circulated in its clipped form. It had been reduced in value but represented what it had originally been. However, for the people using the coin, it bought less. In The United States since about 1913, and certainly since about 1935, money has been a bookkeeping entry at a bank. The United States coined silver until about 1960 and in that form the money had intrinsic value.

The Federal Reserve Board, to which Congress delegated the Constitutional duty to maintain a money system, through certain actions such as a discount rate or a deposit requirement, and, lately, by buying bonds, creates the amount of money available to transact business. A bank account, if the Federal Reserve Board increases the amount of credit available, or creates money by buying debt, loses value just as the value of a clipped coin did in former times. When the Federal Reserve Board creates an account in the name of the United States of America at the Federal Reserve Bank of New York, the value of all bank accounts in the United States diminishes. Similarly, the value of all wages, salaries, profits and other forms of remuneration are diminished. Thus, a form of taxation has taken place other than forcible seizure. When the Federal Reserve Bank of New York created a huge deposit in the name of the United States recently, to finance the "stimulus", the people of the US were in that way taxed in the loss of value of their property. There remain many who believe in the economics of deficit spending to promote growth and who care but little for the value of savings of those who provide for their own living.

Five

Nothing as profound as Spengler is suggested, but there is an historical perspective to our present situation. From Solon to Cicero, Western man appears as thoughtfully attempting to present virtue as rational. Those people repeatedly resorted to welfare, but the individual was never completely submerged. After Rome had gradually expanded from a small city state in central Italy to a tenuously powerful area of a little over half of the Italian peninsula, she suddenly conquered the world in 50 years. Men greedy for money, power and public acclaim combined with massive welfare to produce chaos. The forces of tyranny and a man of outstanding ability joined to bring history to a focus. The Senate chose Pompey Magnus as champion of freedom, and Caesar advanced from Gaul upon Rome. Pompey retreated to Dyrrhachium to be defeated near Pharsalus. After Dyrrhachium and Pharsalus, Rome became even larger and more powerful, but individualism passed from Western Civilization for more than 1000 years, and the people of Rome became subject to the unlimited discretion of an emperor called, regardless of his name, Caesar.

After Rome collapsed in the west, the Dark Ages became a time of an intense social view of business, types of welfare and extreme intolerance. There were received opinions, and none others permitted.

Early Modern History records that men slowly began to consider the individual, the Humanists to write as individuals, the Reformation figures gave individualism theological expression and examples of individuals pitted against huge organizations. Ultimately, individuals were considered even in governmental philosophy.

Two fundamental attitudes arose as men thought their way out of monarchy-nobility and into self determination. Those two attitudes are individual liberty as opposed to collectivist sameness.

The people of England had two revolutions before the American Revolution, and those revolutions produced debate of principles of government. The ideas generated were employed in the American opposition to the despotism of England.

Shortly after the American Revolution a revolution occurred in France, in part stimulated by the same ideas.

The English and American Revolutions adopted the individualist ideology. France substituted for its worn out monarchy a despotic committee espousing collectivist slogans and exercising raw power. England and America prospered and France never recovered. (After WWII England imposed upon itself a socialist government which almost destroyed her and now, years later, she still struggles.)

The collectivist ideas fomented by the French Revolution have continued, and their clichés and often repeated phrases have become accepted as first principles, even though they are often contradictory. One overriding precept of the French Revolution as well as the Bolshevik Revolution was the elimination of rights provided to individuals.

Viewed from the standpoint of individuals an unequal distribution of property and income is not a public vice. When one person gains no other person loses except when crime and fraud are involved. Said another way, it costs me nothing for my neighbor to make a lot. Yet, there is a hue and cry that large differences exist between those who earn a lot and those who earn a little as though the gap were, of itself, a public vice. The French Revolution valued equality above liberty, the framers of our Constitution valued liberty above equality.

Viewed from the standpoint of individuals, individual discrimination that does no harm but to sensibilities is not a public vice. To refuse service does no harm, other than hurt feelings. Those refused are free to seek service elsewhere and those who refuse service are themselves deprived of the money to be earned from the service. When the baker refused to make a cake for a homosexual wedding he did no harm but to sensibilities and he, likewise denied himself the profit in the bargain. Those so refused were themselves at liberty to employ another to bake a cake. Even so, individual choice is in the process of punishment.

Six

Before the USA was created, few could conceive of a government not composed of monarchy-nobility. Many of the early advocates such as Locke found it necessary to employ an apologetic idea as a support for the erosion of the absolute rule of the monarch and the privilege of the nobility. Finally the idea that man has the power and right to establish any government which is desired became accepted. By 1776 the idea of absolute rule and special privilege had been abandoned by many thinking people of Western civilization. In this environment the United States of America was born. Our fathers employed all of the modern libertist ideas:

1. Those who execute, administer, the law do not make the law;
2. Those who make law must be numerous but not too numerous; and they must be required to live under the laws which they enact;
3. There must be a limit on the government in certain sensitive areas, such that individuals are not subject to the sovereignty of the government in those areas;
4. There shall be no official classes and special privilege shall not be extended to any person or group.

Why did our fathers employ the four principles above? To safeguard individual liberty.

Ought man to be at liberty or should he be a mere part of a collective? Ought man to be at liberty to succeed or fail or should he be equalized? Ought man to be at liberty to practice what most consider abhorrent so long as he does no harm?

The classical liberal position of liberty and its natural consequences has never been fully and logically adopted. Liberty includes the right to be wrong, and men are intolerant of that.

Liberty includes the sufferance of an individual to fail or succeed, to gain or lose, to work or not to work, to live a healthy life or to poison himself, and many are intolerant of all of these.

Many are unwilling to accept the hard reality of this planet that there will be an unequal distribution of property regardless of the government system. The Soviet Union exemplified this as the officials of the Party gained huge preferences.

There has been a remarkable and irrational ambivalence in America.

There are those who want a government reduced in its power to investigate crime, which permits individual discretion in what one reads or says or does, except when that person holds a prejudice, and who want that same government to have the power to take what one person has gained and redistribute it to another.

There are those who want to decide the use of money they earn but have the government dictate what people can read.

Almost everyone wants to suppress discrimination.

The moral positions of many seem to be threatened by liberty.

There are many who believe that the distribution of property is unfair when it is unequal. It is true that many moral positions are not enforceable in the presence of liberty, and battle arises over just what should be law and what must be mere persuasion.

It is true that liberty results in an unequal distribution of property, and the question arises whether to have liberty or equality. It should also be remembered, equalization always results in the enrichment of those in power above those out of power. It is also true that liberty results in individual discrimination that does no harm, other than hurt feelings.

In America the moral questions are about decided. Abortion and homosexual marriage continue to be debated, though it appears that homosexual marriage has about been accepted by most.

The central issue today is whether the government shall redistribute property or individuals decide what to do with property which they have gained by work or successful risk or from their parents. There exists no issue regarding individual discrimination that does no harm, it is not allowed. There does exist an argument in favor of lawlessness when it takes the form of demonstrations against lawful authority. Destruction of property during demonstrations is normally overlooked by authorities. Rioting is now permitted.

We are no longer arguing over the right of a king and how he came to have the right. We are now engaged in the struggle for men's minds to determine whether the rights of an individual which he came to have by the painful sacrifice of his forebears will be preserved or relinquished to government. Few are fully aware of the great sacrifices of our forebears who created the United States of America. There are many who have no knowledge of the ideas that brought into existence the United States of America, nor even the idea of individual liberty. There are many who are unaware of history and its record of the rise of tyrants. There are many who consider it their right to riot and demolish others property. Such people have the vote.

Tragically to some, gladly to others, the struggle is about done and we are poised to sacrifice individual liberty for collective causes. The recent uproar over the Indiana law that protects actions taken for religious beliefs is but a manifestation of the fact that the people of the United States are on the threshold of accepting a Caesar. The complaint against the law routinely expressed the idea that it could be used to justify discrimination against homosexuals. Of course it was clearly meant to protect those like the baker who refused to bake a wedding cake for a same-sex marriage and faced a lawsuit for having done so even though same sex marriage was offensive to his religious beliefs. The governor wilted in the face of the outcry and it became clear that discrimination was universally condemned.

It was unanimous, no one said that in our so-called free society a person is at liberty to discriminate so long as he does no harm but for hurt feelings. A few came forward to defend "religious liberty". Not one person came forward to defend individual liberty. The condemnation of discrimination became a received position. The acceptance of received positions forebodes the elimination of dissent. A society that welcomes the elimination of dissent is poised to accept a Caesar. Those who despise the present deadlock in government based in differing opinions will applaud the decisiveness of a Caesar.

We are not engaged in a disagreement over business. Business will be transacted as it was under the Stuarts and as it was under the Communist special privilege class in Russia. It remains true, however, that business conducted under liberty has provided the greatest good for the greatest number.

It is no longer liberty or monarchy-nobility but liberty or collectivist sameness. In the near future it will become liberty or Caesar ... and Caesar will win. He always does.

Seven

We are in a very critical point in Western man's struggle from absolute government to self-determination, from subject of an unlimited government to sovereign individual. The sovereign individual, created by the Constitution of the United States, has almost ceased to exist. There are those who assemble and shout, but, they are of no effect. Often they are shouting for repeal of the right to assemble. There are those who defy the law and use drugs. There are many who protest the government listening to or reading their communications. They consider it to be an invasion of a right to privacy. Many of those who so protest favor laws that punish personal prejudice and bring about redistribution of income and wealth. Law abiding men in America are no longer at liberty so long as they do no harm to others. They are being brought into conformity at an accelerated rate.

To an individual it matters not if his liberty, and the self-expression which accompany it, are overwhelmed in the name of stamping out poverty and prejudice and discrimination or in the name of suppression of heresy or what the medieval society saw as obscene profit, or in the name of health insurance for all. If done by king, Congress or Politburo or President, the result will be the same. The right as differentiated from permission will be lost.

Eight

What are rights?

Jeremy Bentham ridiculed Jefferson and his fellow drafters of the Declaration of Independence for the phrase that all men are created equal. All men are manifestly not created equal. Even though all men are not created equal, what rights do any of us actually have? A right to life? Where is that right when a robber executes his victim as he takes his property? A right to freedom of movement? Where is that right in Cuba, Venezuela, China, Iran, Russia? A right to the proceeds of our labor? Where is that right in vast areas of the world including the United States of America? How do we acquire rights, from whence do they arise? Many would argue that rights are bestowed by God, but, that seems to indicate that God is powerless in many places.

Individual liberty is the only basis that ever existed for the right to any of the following as distinguished from the mere sufferance of them to exist:

1. The publication of facts, opinions, attitudes, beliefs, or any other form of idea freely and without fear of penalty for having done it,

2. Traveling both inside and outside the jurisdictional limits of the ruling government,

3. Assembly with others,

4. Making and enforcing contracts,

5. To be entitled to that equation between time, effort and thought, the results of one's work.

All governmental philosophies, other than modern individual liberty, have merely permitted an individual to have any of these things by sufferance of the state of which he was a subject part. Other than the United States of America, all governments have always had the power, exercised or not, to fully control the lives of their citizens.

Many are not aware of the important difference between the right to certain kinds of conduct and to the acquisition and use of property as distinguished from the fact of doing or acquiring. When people have a right to speak and write and publish as they sovereignly see fit, they often do not say what they think because it is better to remain silent. The actual fact of how wealth turns out to be distributed and the right to acquire wealth are not at all the same.

Rights exist by reason of the power incipient within a people to grant those rights to individuals through the exercise of that power. The people can and do revoke rights. The right to private discrimination was revoked by The Civil Rights Act. The right to practice private discrimination has been revoked by unanimous consent. The right to provide for oneself alone was revoked by The Affordable Care Act. It appears that the right to determine how one uses his own time and talent is about to be further proscribed in punishing those who refuse to cooperate in same-sex marriage. It is reported in the press as a result of polls that almost half of the people from age 18 to 35 believe that there should be a law punishing those who offend others sensibilities causing them mental discomfort even by so little as odious language. The right to freedom of speech which is so often adored can easily be revoked.

Nine

It makes sense to decide what one basically wants as regards any endeavor, and this is especially true when we consider what we want our government to be.

To be called government (anything less is anarchy) there must be:

1. The power to maintain sovereign identity,

2. Fix and adjudicate the relations between those within jurisdictional limits,

3. Maintain order and punish for crimes within jurisdictional limits.

Crimes have always been dealt with in a similar fashion. Recently western man has attempted to deal with criminals in a different way, but we still deal with crime the same as man has from out of prehistory. The maintenance of sovereignty is a simple proposition. We must be prepared to fight and do so when necessary. It is in the governmental determination and adjudication of relations between people that men have always and even today still find their differences.

It is arguable that there is any real value in participation in a benevolent government, but there is no room to argue that any government which is benevolent, regardless of who and how many vote, is preferable to any other government which is despotic, regardless of who and how many vote.

Even before Polybius categorized governments as aristocracies, democracies or oligarchies, it was (and continues to be) true that no system affords complete protection of its citizens from despotism, and all those forms of government have, from time to time, been benevolent and despotic.

It has become dogma that democracy produces benevolent government. That is, unfortunately, not true. Democracies have been among the most despotic of governments. The men assembled in Philadelphia in the summer of 1787 sought above all things to avoid democracy. Witness this from Madison's Notes on the Constitutional Convention of 1787:

'Mr. Gerry. The evils we experience flow from the excess of democracy....'

'Mr. Mason ... admitted that we had been too democratic ....'

The despotism that can be wielded by the majority was recognized in Philadelphia in 1787 and provisions were included to prevent the despotism of the majority. It appears that protection of a minority is vanishing from America. Protection of views abhorrent to the majority is vanishing.

If we are seeking benevolent government, we need to determine what is benevolence. Plato's Republic was his concept of a benevolent government, but it never considered individual liberty. Likely Lenin and Stalin and Hitler thought of themselves as benevolent. Hobbes, Locke, Hume, Smith, Burke, Montesquieu, Montaigne and others brought to consideration the idea that individual liberty is the standard by which one may judge whether a governmental action is benevolent or despotic.

Montesquieu's separation of power, Locke's will of the majority limited in its power and the idea that legislators be required to live under the laws they enacted (America has abandoned this idea, and Congress has become an elite separate estate) were all conceived as protections to individual liberty. The Constitution of The United States of America was adopted with individual liberty as the standard by which a government may be adjudged as benevolent.

There has been a gradual and insidious gravitation to collectivism as the standard of benevolence. The gravitation of late has been apace. The so-called issues of our times need to be made clear in terms of these realities rather than shadows.

Communism is a propaganda front for raw power. Capitalism is no more than a name, capital is. Capital is like matter or gravity or energy. State ownership of capital, or the rule of the proletariat are silly ideas. Men own capital and men rule men, and the only protection of the individual is the limitation upon the power of the government. Democracy is a mere form, and if everyone votes and individuals are submerged, there is no less despotism. In a true democracy no protection of individuals or minority groups is possible. For such protection the power of the government must be limited, precisely as provided in Philadelphia in 1787.

The true issues are whether we shall have as our standard of benevolence the liberty of the individual or unlimited government which forces a redistribution of capital, income and choice. Shall we have the sovereign individual or shall individuals be mere pawns of society? Shall we collectivize medical care or permit individuals to seek out medical care as they see fit? Shall education of children be disciplined enlightenment of minds or rearrangement of society? Shall history be viewed as it actually happened or to accomplish social purposes. Shall people be free to seek out their own destinies or shall government engineer them to ordained purposes. Shall the government, voted into power by a majority, be able to bring conformity to the will of that majority, even though the activity of the minority does no harm to others?

Happily for some, sadly for others, we have abandoned individual liberty as our standard of benevolence. We have adopted suppression of discrimination and collectivist programs in which the government acts to provide for individuals and now we are commencing the debate over another step in collectivization, equalization.

Without question many pitiful and tragic situations exist in America. Every person in America would like to alleviate all of the tragedies in our society. Can we have a perfect society? Is a perfect society the goal, and if it is, what is the attribute of a perfect society? Is a perfect society one in which individuals are free to seek their own destiny or is it one in which pitiful situations are eliminated? If a perfect society is the elimination of pitiful circumstances, the power necessary to achieve perfection must be such as to eliminate slothfulness, ignorance, bigotry, fear, despair, hatred, and personal greed and ambition. Just such power passed from Czar to Politburo to Chairman to President in Russia, but, the result could hardly be termed benevolence.

Once we have accepted collectivist government as actor, actor in social change, in economic distribution, in cultural attitudes, we have forsaken our right to individual liberty. We have enacted many laws which make the government such an actor. To a great extent we have forsaken our right to individual liberty. As the press often reports, it is popular to thus forsake individual liberty. As history reports, such a government is poised to accept a Caesar.

To those who created the United States of America the best guiding principle for deciding what a government should be and what it should do is that man ought to be at liberty. Not that there ought to be a more equal society or better distribution of property or an elimination of poverty and prejudice, or medical care for all. There are none in America who would not want to see an elimination of poverty and prejudice. The elimination of poverty and prejudice is a great undertaking for a person or group if it is accomplished by persuasion and by changing men's minds. If the guiding principle of government is individual liberty, it is despotism if it is accomplished by the force of government.

Ten

Social Gain.

The modern libertist society inherited a social system.

The idea of social gain addressed itself to surviving ancient and medieval forms and the modern state, after first abolishing classes, addressed itself to these broad categories:

1. The protection of children

2. The abolition of slavery

3. Individual redress for injury

4. The right of labor to organize

5. Money system changes

6. The accumulation of wealth

The idea of liberty is that man ought to be free to act volitionally to the extent that he does not invade another. Stated another way, man ought to be at liberty and in order to be at liberty he must be protected by the strength of society from the invasion of others who may be more powerful either physically or socially. Society protects itself from criminals in order that it might be free to pursue private goals without the almost enslaving necessity of individual self protection.

Prior to the modern libertist society children were mere chattels of their parents. Children are people, powerless people, not mere chattels of their parents. They are entitled to equal protection of the strength of society. They are entrusted to their parents who act as very interested representatives of society while the child is yet unable to act for himself. If the parent is unfit to act for society to provide protection for the child, he is removed as the supervisor of the child. Thus, child labor laws, and free public education required by law and paid for by all. Tragically public education paid for with taxes has become predominantly an exercise in futility. There has been no consensus to explain why, only the observation that children of well to do families fare better in our educational system and in our economy. More of this later, but, experts tell us that the ability to function in our present society is determined by age three.

If a person is injured either physically or as a result of damage or destruction of property, he must have a means for compensation (to be returned to the former position) if he is to be protected in his person from others, else the very idea of liberty is lost. One is not free at all if he is left at the whim of others, and he must be always on the defensive or seeking out his own redress. Such a thing is mere chaos

Slavery, a social form from out of pre-history, survived into the creation of the modern libertist state. The libertist quickly began the movement to abolish it. In a society based upon individual liberty, slavery, antithetical to that basis, cannot be permitted. Slavery, as a practical matter, was intellectually abolished by 1776 and the delay in practice is merely the delay in which men engage in all of their affairs.

The Constitutional Convention had many present opposed to slavery as a practice. Many in the South recognized the illegitimacy of slavery. Many in the South could not afford to own a slave. Slavery was permitted to continue for a while, ended in a bitter, senseless war, and continues to haunt us to this day. But, as we see in analysis of our system, slavery can exist in many forms. It is hateful in any form.

The right of men to organize in any way was not seriously questioned, but the organization and bargaining produced the necessity for rules to maintain order. The violence of those early labor-owner disputes is a sad commentary upon the irrationality of man.

From out of the distant past the manipulation of money to accomplish social purposes has been repeated frequently and our early libertist society soon began to also consider changes in the money system which it inherited from the medieval society. Money soon becomes the only form of capital which is a practical means of commencing gain. For this reason a stable money system makes it more difficult for those who start life with little capital to obtain an accumulation. Stated another way, if you have little it is hard to get started. A stable money system functions to protect the established accumulation of capital, but, it does make it more difficult for those with little to start with to get started.

The manipulation of the money system has also brought inroads into the individual liberty that Americans once enjoyed. Wealth and money are not the same. Money is merely a medium of exchange while wealth consists of objects and ideas that produce the means by which people survive and prosper. A few examples render the understanding of the concept easy.

First let us examine the most fundamental of the examples of wealth, land. It may be used to construct buildings which produce income from rent. The income need not be in money, but it has become so that it now is in the form of money. That money can then be exchanged for food and clothing and shelter. Once such necessities are satisfied it may become travel and entertainment and savings for the future. Land also may be the basis of the most basic of all commerce. A person prepares land and sows seeds which produce commodities such as wheat. That wheat is harvested and stored. From that storage it is sold to become bread and many other forms of food. The farmer is paid for the wheat in money. The storage facility is paid for its shelter in money. Then traders buy and sell the wheat and realize a profit or loss in money. So long as the money which each takes in can then be used to acquire necessities and luxuries its value permits the commerce in wheat to continue. However, money can exist in many forms. For a long time in America it existed in the form of gold and silver. Now it exists in the form of a bookkeeping entry in the electronics of a computer. So long as the electronics of the computer represent the wheat then the money retains its value.

However, when the electronics of the computer are manipulated to some other purpose other than to represent the wheat, that is to say, for instance, to permit the government to write a check to send to a person who is out of work, then the money which the farmer and the storage facility and the trader receives has a constantly changing value. It, in other words, can itself, purchase just so much electricity or meat or labor and that amount constantly changes as the manipulation changes. If, for instance, a pound of wheat and an ounce of silver are equal, then the amount of silver available sets the value of a pound of wheat and since there is always a finite amount of silver available, the wheat produced has a reasonably stable value in terms of money. However, when the wheat can be exchanged for a money which is being manipulated for other purposes it has a constantly changing value and can be exchange for food, shelter, clothing, travel, etc. only as the manipulation permits. Since the time and intellect of people produces the wheat and the manipulation is at the command of the government, the people who produced and traded the wheat no longer stand as individuals at liberty, but as the instruments of the government.

Our attempts to have a money system which both protects what people have and to also make it easier for a person with but little capital to get started have occupied much of the debates of America. It would be a marvelous social gain if such a money system could be found. It has proved to be difficult to accomplish.

The present form of credit as money has manifestly not accomplished its stated purpose, to prevent cycles of business activity and low employment.

The present form of money has reduced each person to but a cog in the wheels of government, not an individual at liberty.

It has become almost universally accepted that the government is responsible for having jobs available for those who want them. This prevails regardless of the fact that times change and some are eliminated from the jobs available because they cannot perform them. Circumstances have changed immensely over the life of the United States of America. The value of labor, once great, has been eroded by workers outside the USA who work for less and who businesses have chosen to employ in order to produce at lower prices. This practice has been rewarded by the purchasing public who buy at the better price. Thus the value of time for many has been reduced. Many jobs require abilities not possessed by some.

A huge portion of the population of the USA has failed to take advantage of the educational opportunities offered them and cannot perform at the level now necessary. The government is helpless to change conditions and conditions manifestly overwhelm the ability of the government. The government can take from those who can perform and redistribute to those who cannot. The government can reduce some to a form of slavery.

Except for the USA, all governments have reduced their citizens to a form of slavery. The processes of a government divided into legislative, executive and judicial branches will prove to be too sluggish for those who want their own way right now. The republican form of Rome proved to be too sluggish to adapt to the demands of a grasping populace. Caesar was required and he was willing, and even though the Senate continued to meet, Caesar ruled.

Judging from the past, business cycles must be. There have been efforts to explain why they must be. There have been many efforts to explain how to eliminate business cycles and how to correct a down cycle. To date no one has been able to completely explain why they occur or how to eliminate or ameliorate them. Government spending, advanced by John Maynard Keynes, and many of his modern disciples, has proven to be ineffective, especially today. A people overburdened with their own debt cannot but eliminate that debt before they can create new markets for production. With massive spending already in place, government spending of borrowed or created money has done naught but add to the debt and the reduction in value of the holdings of the people.

A stable money seems the best method to moderate the severity and length of recessions. The people of America have been poorly served by letting them believe that the government will or even can eliminate recessions and their repercussions and, thus, to heap debt upon themselves.

The size and power of the government of the US has been greatly enhanced by propaganda addressed at the elimination and amelioration of recessions. In the process the individual liberty of the people has been reduced. It has become reflexively accepted that the government is responsible for the lives of the people to be pleasant even though government is actually powerless to improve lives. Only individual effort can improve lives. When, by taxation, the government takes from individuals for other than essential governmental functions it reduces them in their ability to improve their lives. When the government operates in a manner that intends to create an environment to bring economic aid to those portions of the populace who are unable to function within the existing economic conditions and purposes to create economic conditions that creates jobs, and leaves the consideration of individual liberty as its basic function, it has already established the basis for accepting Caesar.

Throughout history there have been a few individuals who enjoyed the benefits of very large accumulations of wealth. The social question of huge accumulations of wealth in one person, while there are many who are terribly poor, is better understood in the light of whether it is a form which a modern libertist society can protect under the law. The Jacobins of the French Revolution attempted to abolish private wealth. America decided to adopt the form of private wealth.

England and America could find no harm to any one person for another person to gain a lot, since all of the members of the society are free to pursue gain and realize it if they can.

To the French, if one man gains more than another he has thereby deprived others of that which was more than an equal share. They thought of the economy as a limited whole, not as the product of labor and capital. They could not see what Adam Smith and others advanced, that there is no limit on productivity in a society at liberty and that productivity is the only measure of wealth and the only means of producing wealth.

Eleven

Some argue that gain from nothing other than trading in promises has no productive aspect. Perhaps that is so. In a system at liberty, there is no vice in such trading, the traders, theoretically, face loss as well as gain. It is unjustifiable for governmental interference to exempt such traders from loss.

For one person to gain works no hardship on others. Others are at liberty to gain as well.

In the real world it is true that some prosper above others who work ever so hard, but no collectivist system ever changed that natural state, it only changed the way in which those who prosper achieve their prosperity. There is no way to keep the more able from rising above his less able fellow. The only question is whether the system promotes the ability to prosper as a part of government power, (witness the Soviet Union), or promotes the ability to prosper in commerce.

That which is a social gain in a society whose standard of benevolence is individual liberty is a far different thing from that which is a social gain in a society in which collectivist sameness is the standard of benevolence. The almost universal acceptance of the idea that discrimination is wrong and should be punished shrieks that the people of the USA require uniformity. Uniformity is inimical to individual liberty. Uniformity is fertile ground for a Caesar.

People and people alone can produce and a government must tax its citizens in order to exist. The government exercises the power which is incipient in the great number of its citizens, and which is turned over to it by those citizens, to take from those citizens the amount necessary to function. When a government takes from a citizen to protect that citizen from invasion from others and from enslavement by foreign states, to provide a judicial system and a money system, a fire protection system, a police system then, taxes are a necessary cost of liberty.

When a government exercises its power to tax and takes from one to give to another, in a government in which individual liberty is the standard of benevolence, those taxes are not a cost of liberty. They are the operation of collectivist sameness. They are the operation of a form of slavery.

A better money system is a far different thing from the present inflationary practice of our government. Of course, the ultimate effect of ever cheapening the money is to destroy the value of all property, to, in fact, destroy commerce. Although it has become prosaic to refer to it, the Weimar Republic of post-WWI Germany is a perfect example of inflation that destroyed a country, and the result was Hitler and the Nazis.

The operation of the modern welfare state has so impoverished the governments who have resorted to it that they cannot afford to support a military to defend themselves. Sweden, Denmark, Norway, France and to a great extent, Great Britain have all become weak and unable to defend themselves from a militarized government. They are but easy targets for the militant Muslims. They are without the means to join in a fight against militant Muslims. The United States has come to that very circumstance and survives on borrowed money and inflation of its money supply. Medicare, Medicaid and the Affordable Care Act have taken such a huge portion of the produce of the country that the government can no longer afford to adequately pay the Judges of the judicial system. The government has taken from the Social Security Trust fund to the extent that it exists only by reason of a government IOU which it cannot pay but for inflation of the money system.

The operation of the Veterans Administration has become a disgrace and it increasingly appears that the government cannot afford to care for its wounded veterans. But for the recent successes of radical Muslims the defense budget would be dangerously cut because there is not enough government income to support it. Reduction in defense spending was underway when the radical Muslims suddenly began to succeed. The cost of the bombing in Iraq and Syria is paid through borrowing and cheapening of our money. The cost of The Affordable Care Act is paid for with borrowed money and the cheapening of our money. The government is pursuing an agreement with Iran which cannot but lead to Iran having atomic weapons because the government is weak and cannot afford to be strong, nor has it the will.

Twelve

What is social justice?

The libertist says that social justice is the operation of individual liberty. Liberty distributes property on the idea that it is an extension of the person who works for it.

The "progressive" is saying that a person is entitled to an equitable share of the entire produce of the country without regard to individual effort, talent, or even the protection of himself from debilitating life styles.

Is it fair to distribute property on the basis of individual effort and risk?

Is it fair to distribute property on the basis that people are alive?

If one says that it is just to distribute property as a result of individual effort but not just to permit too much accumulation, in the presence of those with too little, how do we decide how much is too much? Who or what group among us is so wise as to be able to fairly determine how much is too much or too little? Is Congress so wise and beneficent that it would not abuse that power? If we did place such power in Congress how long would we differ from slaves in the traditional sense? As we have experienced over the past 50 years, Congress is fully capable of abusing power. We have already explored examples of Congress subverting individuals to its purposes. Russia placed just such power in the hands of the government and the Soviet Union suppressed its people and collapsed from such oppression.

Western man slowly learned tolerance as he came out of the Dark Ages. Tolerance was an ideological necessity which, until recently, was a part of social justice in the modern libertist society. Sadly, today, "progressives" have abandoned tolerance because it permits too many things that "progressives" cannot abide. Everyone should read the tiny book of three essays entitled *A Critique of Pure Tolerance*. Tolerance would permit a cake maker to decide who he chooses to serve. Such tolerance is not permissible in a society controlled by received opinion.

Such tolerance is not acceptable in a society controlled by collectivism.

Compassion was the cry regarding welfare to the so-called ghettos. The welfare did nothing to change the attitudes of those who were said to be trapped in the ghettos, but it destroyed family identity and the will to work, to improve. The War on Poverty has been rejected even by the "progressives" who championed it. President Clinton proudly proclaimed the end of the War on Poverty with the exclamation, "the end of welfare as we have known it". And yet, even as they admit the failure of the huge welfare distribution of the '60s, they continue to strive for more.

Welfare has destroyed every society which has resorted to it. Welfare destroyed Athens and Rome. Welfare brought England to it knees. Welfare destroys the will of the recipient and his own self-esteem. Welfare is in the progressive act of destroying the United States of America. Welfare has always been the lead indicator of a coming tyranny. History reveals it time and again.

Those who write for the press are fond of the idea of a middle ground which accepts inroads into individual liberty. It is reported that Medicare, Medicaid and Social Security are overwhelmingly popular. So let it be. Those programs are on the cusp of failing for lack of funds. There are none who dare to mention the imminent failure of those programs. They appear, however, but precursors to more collectivist programs. The uproar over the inequality of incomes and wealth produce a call for equalization in almost every edition of the press of the country. Frequently the demand is for taxation to bring in more money for the government to spend on education. There are proposals by prominent politicians to increase taxes on upper incomes in order to spend on social programs.

While spending more on education is sought, investigators tell us that a person's place in the distribution of wealth is decided by the age of three. They tell us of the importance of exposure to expanded vocabulary and to literature. They tell us of the necessity of parental involvement. They tell us of the importance of parents reading to children. They do not tell us how parents who can but barely read themselves might be able to read to their children. They do not tell us just how money spent on education can overcome the first three years of deprivation. They do not approach the question of deprivation, they just observe it to exist. One must consider just how money could overcome the deprivation. Those who seek money for additional education seek it for preschool exposure. They do not, however, advocate removing one, two and three-year olds from their families. None have, so far, advocated schools for one, two and three-year olds. Those who advocate more money for education do not tell us just how more money can change a child who refuses an education and who disrupts classes and intimidates teachers. They do not tell us just how more money spent on education can eliminate gangs from schools.

Because advocates of individual liberty began the movement for universal education paid for with taxes, no resistance to taxes for education is rational for the libertist, only a resistance to waste. Few do not believe that better teachers produce better educated children. Just how to evaluate teachers is fiercely debated. An important question arises, are there sufficient persons willing to teach who are able to teach at a higher level to produce better students. Perhaps an increase in pay for teachers would attract more able people, but, how to differentiate between good and not so good teachers eludes us.

The vast inequality in the possession of wealth exists because some are able to buy and sell profitably, it is questionable how education might be able to increase the ability to buy and sell successfully.

Many see the ease of wealth and the difficulty of poverty and cry out for a better distribution. Many see the brutishness of personal prejudice and cry out for its eradication. They are impatient with liberty and want to bring these good things to society right now. Many object to "pure tolerance".

Tragically, history tells us that a government with the power to eradicate poverty, prejudice, excessive wealth and tolerance uses that power to stamp out opposition to itself. History tells us that when a large portion of the populace becomes lawless, restrictions on the power of government are cast aside.

What is social justice? Could it be the freedom and tolerance of individual liberty!

Thirteen

Our Constitution has been partly set aside because of the Great Depression. There have been many explanations for its cause and by now it is widely believed that the Great Depression was caused by Federal Reserve Board money policy. Regardless of the cause or severity of the Great Depression, can we set aside limited government for economic reasons and remain free? Had a patrician landowner been told of the coming Caesars in 100 BC they would have scoffed. Had the free citizens of Athens been told in 500 BC of the coming tyrants they would have scoffed. Had a farmer in Iowa in 1890 been told of the coming invasions of the individual liberties of the people of the USA he would have scoffed.

The acquisition of money, it turns out, is the result of the ability to function within any existing system. In all totalitarian systems the ability to gain is roughly equivalent with the ability to gain favor with the power or to become the power. In liberty the ability to gain is roughly equivalent to the ability to function within the commercial system.

When President Carter made his energy speech he openly espoused the confiscation of oil. If the Congress has the power to enact a tax which represents the difference between the price it fancies to permit an owner of oil to receive and the fair market price of that oil, what is to prohibit a law which sets the price of anything and confiscates all above that price by means of a tax? There is a specific constitutional provision which prohibits the taking of property without a fair price being paid.

Property has a fair market price, which is the price a willing seller will take and willing buyer will give. This fair market price is an inseparable part of all property. When a price is fixed by the government, it has taken part of the property. It is not a very big step from confiscating oil as was done during the Carter administration to confiscating homes. Homes were collectivized in The Soviet Union. When the collectivist monster has devoured oil, it is pretty chancy where it will next make its selection.

Redistribution has become a word so often used that it has almost lost its impact. Every news paper every day has some mention of redistribution. Many TV programs discuss it at length. Movements come and go advocating so called conservatism. Conservatives lost the election in 2008 and 2012 by a landslide. The winners have been moving toward their stated goals just as one could easily predict. The winners have been moving apace at redistribution. As the winners have done as they said they would, a hue and cry has come up from many. Demonstrations have been common.

History tells us that hysterical cries have little effect. When a people have no regard for their liberty, and great regard for their pocket books, redistribution easily sells. When people fail to see themselves as used by politicians and collectivists and fail to see themselves as partial slaves, they are easy prey for collectivists and redistribution. Collectivism cannot be bested with economic arguments, too many care only for what the government does for them. The "progressive" agenda from 1900 until now has been successful on the basis of what people thought it would do for them. It is necessary for those who value liberty to recognize that there are many who do not, who care only for what they might get from government.

Another development which presages a Caesar has arisen in the attack upon The United States by the militant Muslims both from within and without. It calls for a President who can act as a commander-in-chief since it calls for a military response. Our system has been poor in selecting a competent commander-in-chief. Much incompetency and politically driven decisions have been evident since the turn of the 20th century. It would serve little purpose to rehearse the many instances of incompetence, but the latest demonstration by the president is glaring. The incompetence has demonstrated itself as utter fecklessness. The latest attack by militant Muslims which killed 14 people and wounded several more in California occurred as the president dithered about the faltering of the Islamic State.

The present slate of candidates is woefully lacking in any reasonable expectation of competency as a commander-in-chief and altogether glaring in the likelihood of political decisions. Political decisions are driven by current events rather than cold calculating objectivity. That militant Muslims seek the overthrow of The United States could not be more obvious and the likelihood of a military response driven by politics could not be more obvious. As poor military decisions based on politics manifests itself in poor results and militant Muslims become increasingly threatening, the rise of Caesar becomes more imminent.

To have a constitutional limit upon the government there must be a people who want to be sovereign individuals. There can be no constitution unless the people want one. The Constitution itself provides a means of abolishing its own existence and the ideas which produced our constitution provided that a people can have such government as they may choose.

In order to have a constitution, and individual liberty we must be willing to be sovereign individuals. We must be willing to support ourselves. We must be willing to tolerate our fellow citizens. We must be willing to suffer others to succeed while we ourselves do not. We must be unwilling to take from others under the power of the government. We must choose that man ought to be at liberty. We must be persuaded by something other than "what will you do for me?". There must be, at least, a majority, who are willing to support themselves.

The mere fact that the power vested in the government has not been used does not mean that it will not be used.

We have addressed The Affordable Care Act earlier. Proponents of the law say that it is required because the portion of America's production dedicated to medical care is too much. Members of Congress and the President are so saturated with their dominion over the people that they grasp the power to dictate to what people may direct their own money. The proposal speaks eloquently of loss of freedom and increase in power.

How could it be a problem to a free society that they choose how and how much of their income they spend on anything they see fit? It is only a problem in a directed society. It is a problem for The United States because of two massive welfare programs which are on course to bankrupt the government. Of course, the government won't be bankrupt, it will simply create money. In creating money it runs the risk of a repeat of the Weimar Republic.

To control the cost of medical care the power to decide medical care must be taken from individuals and redirected to government bureaucrats.

The people of the U.S. do, indeed, spend much of their produce on medical care. They have done so voluntarily and likely because they place value upon it. Medical care has increased in cost. Likely the increase resulted from many new treatments and diagnostic methods. For every treatment and diagnostic method there is a cost and that cost would not have been incurred but for an anticipated profit. Eliminate the profit and the new medicines, machines and methods will disappear. The cost of medical care will decline. So shall excellent medical care. America has had the finest medical care ever to exist. That resulted from but one thing, the motivation for profit. When that motivation is reduced the excellence of medical care will decline.

It is now reported that the Affordable Care Act is succeeding in its stated goal, ie, to increase the number of people with health insurance. It is also reported that the cost of health insurance for those who already had it has increased. Of course the cost increased because those people have been forced to pay for the insurance for those who have health problems, in many cases because of unhealthy lifestyles. Through the subsidies provided by the government, it also increased the cost of government which must be paid by those same people who have had their insurance costs increased. The subsidies to those unable to pay and paid by the government increase the tax load on those who already were the ones who paid for the operation of the government.

There are additional taxes levied by the Affordable Care Act and paid by those who ordinarily pay taxes. It is common to read that The Affordable Care Act has succeeded and many more people are insured than before its passage. That is exactly what was intended and that is exactly what had to happen. However, many millions of America have been deprived of a portion of their earnings and a portion of their individual liberty. They can assemble and speak, they can send emails and other messages, but, they must pay regardless of their speeches.

The Affordable Care Act also starkly demonstrates the collectivization of the United States. It creates a collective of the entire population and requires that those who are healthy pay for the cost to care for those who are unhealthy. Some approve of the collectivization, we're all in this together, one for all and all for one, and so on. Collectivization necessarily prohibits individual liberty just as has been provided in the Affordable

Care Act. Personal choice cannot survive alongside collectivization.

The stabilization of the price of wheat became more important than Mr. Filburn's personal choice. The elimination of discrimination became more important than the personal choice of Lester Maddox. As the price of wheat became a collective problem, wheat was embargoed. Some people who refuse to participate in same sex marriage have been sued for that reason alone.

Unfortunately the President and many members of Congress are acting out before our eyes that government will exercise the power given it. It is reported that the United States government has begun intervening in litigation on no other basis than that it sees itself as the protector of a portion of society that it finds needy.

Fourteen

Can the mechanism of passing from a collectivist minded Congress elected by the people to a tyranny, as has happened time and again, be foreseen? One obvious way it might occur arises in the present deadlock in the Congress. The press and media report that a huge portion of Americans sees the deadlock as the most important issue of the times. A magnetic demagogue could easily persuade a huge segment of the people to grant to him the power to govern to the tiniest detail of life, and, in the process, eliminate the deadlock and personal choice. One obvious way is that rioting becomes endemic and a magnetic demagogue is required to suppress it. America has seen many examples of magnetic demagogues (Huey Long, Andrew Jackson).

The present deadlock in Congress forms the basis for many to criticize the present system. The present division of opinion and preferences within the population which produces a divided and obdurate Congress which demands that one side give way to the other and cannot agree upon any course of action may well provide the intellectual basis for the acclamation of Caesar.

President Obama, impatient with Congress to enact what he believes to be good, has demonstrated that tyranny is possible in America. Almost every President has demonstrated that he chafes under the restraints of the Constitution and has employed so called executive orders to bring about his desires without the restraint of Congress. Mr. Obama has exceeded them all, and threatens more. The President, by fiat, creating law. A Greek tyrant would applaud.

The people who created the United States of America were able to foresee the demolition of dedication to liberty and thus limited the right to vote. It has become sacrosanct that everyone have the right to vote regardless of their qualifications. Judging from numerous interviews shown on television there are huge numbers of people eligible to vote who have no knowledge of history, civics, or even the name of the sitting president. Such people have no regard whatever for individual liberty. They care for the satisfaction of their immediate wants. They are ripe for the establishment of Caesar.

Mr. Obama has reached an agreement with Iran without any debate or consideration by Congress. He somewhat changed his position and agreed that Congress may have some input into any such agreement, but, that has not changed his attitude, the agreement proceeds and Congress is impotent. He appears at present to be on a course to punish Israel because of his animosity toward Benjamin Netanyahu. He clearly is intent upon acting without any restraint. He has declared that he will veto any act of Congress that refuses to abide his decision. Many approve.

The humane sentiment which formed the basis for simple assistance to the helpless has given way to more and greater demands for more and broader powers in the government and for more and deeper erosion of the sovereign individual. It is not as though the loss of liberty were a mere prospect which threatened in the future, it has long since been in the process of happening. The demand for increased assistance for the unsuccessful arises in the increase in population and the inevitable increase in the unsuccessful. So long as labor remained valuable the demand remained muted. The reduction in the value of labor produces an increase in the number of unsuccessful. Demand for assistance for the unsuccessful will ultimately, as it has time and again, arouse a cry to eliminate the restrictions on the power of the government and the rise of Caesar.

An eerie feeling of unreality accompanies the slip to tyranny, but, history graphically pictures it; a government that acts to perpetuate itself in place of social rearrangement.

The planet on which we live has some harsh rules. Equality in any aspect of life except before the law cannot be provided and individual liberty alone stands in the way of despotic government.

If one does not have the right to the result of his work and risk, what rights has he in the presence of a government so powerful that it can take from a person the very equivalent of his time, energy and intellect? If one has no right to carry out his own ideas in practice, so long as he does not invade others, what rights has he in the presence of a government so powerful that it can proscribe conduct which is not consistent with the received position as expressed by king or Congress or Politburo or Chairman or President, or even a majority of the people? If people who do not want to buy insurance can be forced to buy it against their will, just what limit exists upon a government so powerful? If people want to join with others who lead a healthful life to buy health insurance at a cost that reflects that healthy lifestyle and are prohibited that choice, what limits exist upon the government to force its choice upon the people. The limits upon the power of the government intended to protect individual liberty have been eroded to the point that they no longer exist. It will be but a small step to welcome Caesar.

The limitation of the power of the government was a paramount thought in the creation of the Constitution of the United States of America. Collectivist government cannot tolerate limited government. Collectivists do not see limits on government as a virtue. The "progressives" have told us that the government is us. That is tragically false.

Man has always had the innate idea that he could arrive at a general theory of truth and a perfect society. One thing stands out in history and that is that received opinions cause severe despotism. In a perfect society received opinions are a necessity, it would not be perfect if different ideas were acceptable. The people of this country innately think that we should eliminate all of the bad things in it. No argument for the continuation of anything bad in America could be defended. However, individual liberty, if it is not a perfect society, is the best society of which man has until now been capable. Collectivism has demonstrated its horrible imperfections time and again.

Can a democracy exercise the responsibility of foresight? Must we wait until it is too late? Could we again give first consideration to liberty instead of equalized distribution or planned society or the elimination of discrimination? Although there are many who would not, surely most people who are given the opportunity to see it will understand that if a person no longer has the right to decide the use of his earnings, can be forced to buy insurance, he has, in the same transaction, lost all rights and is once again at the sufferance of government. The problem arises in "the opportunity to see it". It is almost impossible to place the ideas before the people, they mostly are bored with it.

What difference that the government is no longer a king, but has been replaced by another form with power to decide what it will suffer its subjects. Tragically, history tells us that the form of government which ultimately comes to power is the rise of a Caesar.

We have never had a class to whom it devolved as a duty to preserve the republic. It is the task of every person who loves liberty. Everyone should read Locke's *Second Treatise on Civil Government* and Mill's *On Liberty*. Everyone should read Madison's *Notes on the Constitutional Convention of 1787*. Everyone should read Friedrich Hayek, Ludwig Von Mises, Jefferson and Adams letters, Adam Smith, and the list goes on. Everyone should read the tiny book of three essays entitled *A Critique of Pure Tolerance,* which describes how tolerance permits such hated things as private discrimination.

It is unlikely to be so.

Yet, the innate good sense of many of the people of the US could see, if presented to them, the truth in liberty as the test of benevolence. It is unlikely to succeed in terms of economic arguments. While true that liberty has been the driving force behind an economy that produced the greatest abundance to the greatest number, only a portion, likely a minority, can be expected to appreciate that fact as a compelling argument. Only a few would fail to appreciate what life lived under tyranny would mean. Perhaps people under unlimited tyrants enjoyed that life. It is now revealed that many in Russia openly seek a return to The Soviet Union. History reveals bloody wars to throw off tyranny. The ability to foresee such a calamitous event is a problem. As it happens, that tyranny, if not from a Caesar but from a Congress, exists right now. It appears that but few see it. It is inevitable that unlimited power in an elected Congress will gravitate to a tyrant who, then, as Thucydides tells us, will act for his own benefit.

The "progressive" seeks to spread the wealth around to people who do not have it, and at the same time they will not have a right to keep it, only a sufferance to keep what the Congress sees fit to permit. "Progressives" do not see the threat to freedom of expression and assembly. Many do not feel the immediacy of the loss of liberty. Many take to the streets with shouts and fire and believe that they are at liberty. Owners of oil felt it when their property was confiscated under Nixon and Carter, owners of grain felt the collectivist power when the government embargoed grain. Those who might choose to forego medical insurance will feel it under the present law. The healthy have already experienced it under present law as their cost for medical care has increased. As the list grows so does the power in the government and the ability to regain liberty reduced. A sovereign individual, seen as radical by many, will become seditious.

Fearfully, one must consider that when Karl Marx predicted the inevitability of collectivism he had it right.

Liberty is not easy.

Mill closes *On Liberty* with these words:
"A State which dwarfs its men, in order that they may be more docile instruments in its hands even for beneficialpurposes – will find that with small men no great thing can really be accomplished; and that the perfection of machinery to which it has sacrificed everything will in the end avail it nothing, for want of the vital power which, in order that the machine might work more smoothly, it has preferred to banish."

Who can argue with compassion and sharing? More pertinent, who can or who will argue with a government of absolute power and committed to received opinion? We read in almost every edition of the papers of America of the imprisonment of those who criticize the powers that control China. Harry Elmer Barnes in his mammoth task, *An Intellectual and Cultural History of the Western World*, wrote:

> "The human race has been extremely intolerant of dissent and novelty. Countless thousands, since the dawn of history, have come to an untimely end or have endured excruciating tortures because they have dared to think or act in opposition to the majority. A heavy penalty has been placed upon nonconformity."

Collectivist government cannot permit deviation from its purposes and, therefore, cannot permit individual liberty for the reason that liberty permits nonconformity. The penalties imposed through the force of government is tragedy upon a grand scale; it is despotism.

Walter Isaacson, in his excellent biography of Albert Einstein, quotes the great discoverer: "The development of science and the creative activities of the spirit requires a freedom that consists in the independence of thought from the restrictions of authoritarian and social prejudice."

When a majority, even though a huge majority, acting upon received opinion, is able to suppress an activity that causes no harm other than hurt feelings, the very spirit that brought about the United States of America is lost and "the freedom that consists in the independence of thought from the restrictions of authoritarian and social prejudice," has been so fundamentally infringed that received opinion once again rules just as it did in Medieval times.

There is little question that it was that individual liberty at work in America which brought about the United States of America, the only government to ever exist with its very purpose to guarantee to each individual his liberty and to adopt a system dedicated to that purpose. It has sheltered millions who escaped from totalitarian regimes. It has provided the opportunity for millions to improve their lives. It has created a system to produce the greatest good to the greatest number.

The United States of America is in danger of collapse from excessive spending on collectivist schemes. It is facing collapse from efforts to equalize. It is facing catastrophic transformation. It is unlikely that any government "so conceived and so dedicated" might arise in its place as it was utterly unique in the history of man.

There were Aristocrats and Democrats, rich and poor, at Philadelphia. They achieved a compromise to safeguard individual liberty, ie., limited government. Now that government is beset with greed for wealth, power, and public acclaim, coupled with massive welfare and received opinions. If the focus of 48 BC is not present, it is near. The forces of tyranny are in view for those who care to see. As yet there is no clear Caesar, though he awaits with a promise to act on behalf of the people. Lovers of liberty pray for a better champion than Pompey.

To paraphrase the incomparable Saint Paul: The day of liberty is far spent. The night of collectivism is at hand.

Epilogue

Throughout the foregoing study I have avoided the personal pronoun 'I'. Permit me this brief personal observation.

I have been a student of the United States for 75 years. At first, despite the influence of my family, I was an unapologetic "progressive". The past 60 years have revealed an understanding of the steady drift away from liberty and toward collectivism.

I have written the foregoing in a hope, however dim, that some younger Americans might come to an understanding of the immense loss we are suffering and come to the aid of our failing Republic which is dreadfully poised to pass from a democracy to a tyranny. The Republic was never meant to become a democracy and as it has done so it has also adopted the course of many democracies before it. There are those who believe that the ideas and words from 240 years ago are no longer appropriate for today. Those words and ideas, however, are eternal and have never become outdated. On the following page is a small reading list for those unacquainted with the eternal ideas that created the United States of America. We can but pray that an arousal of the love of liberty which one may find in these volumes might again light the torch of liberty in the only government ever dedicated to it.

Reading List

The Cambridge Ancient and Medieval Histories

The Decline and Fall of the Roman Empire, Gibbon.

A Military History of the Western World, Fuller

The Histories of Polybius

The History of the Peloponnesian Wars, Thucydides

The writings of John Locke, Montaigne, Montesquieu, Edmund Burke, Adam Smith

Notes on the Constitutional Convention of 1787, Madison

The Adams and Jefferson Letters

Herodotus, The Histories

The Mainspring of Human Progress, Henry Grady Weaver

The surviving portions of histories by Livy, Tacitus, Suetonius,

Portions of the writings of Cicero

On Liberty, John Stuart Mill

The writings of: Ludwig Von Mises, Friedrich Hayek, Thomas Sowell and Walter Williams

There are so many histories of the American revolution that to name but a few would be presumptuous, however, try *Ideological Origins of the American Revolution*, Gordon Wood

www.ingramcontent.com/pod-product-compliance
Lightning Source LLC
Chambersburg PA
CBHW071253280526
45788CB00004B/1696